My Journey Thru "L"*
*Lymphoma

BACKGROUND

From January 2005 thru the present (May 2006), I have had itchy spots moving around the ole body. Here is my story of diagnosis and treatment. Sure, I've had cancer once before (prostate – with seed implant, three years ago) and hip replacement (ten years ago) and open-heart surgery (five by- passes twenty years ago), but it seems this may require a longer-term treatment and be a trek worth tracing.

In journaling this journey, I plan to record each day as it comes and not go back for rewording or reworking. The trip should be interesting, revealing, and, for me, challenging.

The doctors and staff are the travel directors.

Start the engines!!

-Bill Castle

My Journey Thru "L" *

*Lymphoma

by patient, patient Bill Castle

iUniverse, Inc.
New York Bloomington

My Journey Thru "L" *
*Lymphoma

iUniverse books may be ordered through booksellers or by contacting:

iUniverse
1663 Liberty Drive
Bloomington, IN 47403
www.iuniverse.com
1-800-Authors (1-800-288-4677)

Because of the dynamic nature of the Internet, any Web addresses or links contained in this book may have changed since publication and may no longer be valid. The views expressed in this work are solely those of the author and do not necessarily reflect the views of the publisher, and the publisher hereby disclaims any responsibility for them.

ISBN: 978-1-4401-1220-1 (sc)
ISBN: 978-1-4401-1221-8 (ebook)

Printed in the United States of America

iUniverse rev. date: 1/2/2009

Disclaimer:

All physician and medical personnel names have been changed to
protect their privacy.
Friends and family have given permission for the use of their names.

In loving memory of Bill Castle, who brightened the lives of his family and friends and countless others that crossed his path.

And my thanks to those who helped me publish his poetic journal.

~Sue Castle

PLANNING FOR THE TRIP OF TREATMENTS

May 5-7, 2006

This is the weekend before first infusion,
Destined to straighten out all my confusion,
All of my itching and scratching galore
That's lasted 4 months and a year, if not more.

My own family's worried, concerned, or not knowing.
Shoulda seen me last Thursday when I was a-glowing
From nuclear MUGA scan lighting the chart,
Trying to find out the strength of my heart.

It still is the weekend before first infusion
And thinking of past months is rather amusing.
None of my doctors could figure me out –
'Twasn't allergies, eczema – all were in doubt.

When out of a lab there arose such a question:
"Should we test blood again?" What a marvelous suggestion!"
And throw in a CAT scan and body scan to boot.
We gotta find out what's wrong with this coot."

Finally in March came the real diagnosis.
Said good Dr. "C", "You don't have psychosis.
What you have now is a low-grade lymphoma".
I jumped up and hugged him, almost gave him a diploma.

(Cont'd)

Now we know what I'm facing and even its name:
Non-Hodgkins Lymphoma is what we can blame.
So on with the treatment, the chemo – let's go,
Let's tackle this monster and then overthrow.

I'm already getting cards "Thinking of you".
Maybe they know a lot more than I do.
And people at church are praying for me.
Makes me feel good – what a great family!

I almost forget other problems I had –
My legs are below me (for that I am glad)
But left leg is short and needed a lift,
It's kept me from walking my usual swift.

So a lift in the heel and a rocker on the shoe
With physical therapy in March did I do.
Then out on the tennis court time after time
Came a pain in right knee cap – and it was mine.

"See Dr Vantini and get the thing fixed."
So arthroscopic knee surgery, between and betwixt.
Then CAT scans and blood tests and biopsy, too!
(I'm beginning to think I belong in a zoo).

When April appeared, we took Florida vacation.
Needed rest and relaxing for fortification.
But now we are ready for whatever may come –
Me and my Suzie, my super-special chum.

WEEK 1

Monday, May 8

We met this morn with Dr "C"
Who wanted to explain to me
The six-month treatment that we face
And all the ifs and ands – "in case".

He said my lymphoma was at moderate growth,
Made me sign-up for the 'Be Good Boy' oath.
The stage of disease, he called it 2A,
A moderate spread thru my body of decay.

So the next three hours were spent in a chair
With TV, coffee, donuts there.
Friendly nurses by the dozen
Hooked up drip-bag called Rituxan.

Its job: help the immune system fight
Those infected old B cells causing my plight.
They all gave me warning how 'crappy' I'll get
But up thru tonight – no problems. Not Yet!

Tuesday, May 9

This morning while shaving I nicked my old chin
And blood spurted out all over my skin
So a bandage I wore when I walked thru the door.
The nurses exploded and reeled off a roar.

Back for my second day of infusion
(They promised the coming days won't be amusin')
'Twas a series of drugs they politely call CHOP
All designed to make growth of the cancer cells stop.

It took just two hours, with donut hole in hand.
These procedures and drugs I'm learning first hand.
It's great to have Sue sitting there by my side.
Don't know what I'd do without my sweet bride.

I felt pretty good the rest of the day,
Phone calls from friends sure are great, aren't they?
Side effects are few yet, 'cept hiccups and wet pants.
None are serious 'but give it a chance'.

Wednesday, May 10

Day 3 ends this series of infusion with a shot
To build up white blood cells before they all rot.
The nurses were upbeat, all competent and nice.
I asked lotsa questions, they gave good advice.

I felt pretty good throughout the whole day
Though my tongue-taster's slipping and fading away.
My hiccups were on and off all the day long,
Kind of a bother but I just sing along.

Had enough energy to put up the screens
But Sue's wearing down from my medical scenes.
She smiles most the time taking care of my life
Don't know what I'd do without my dear wife.

Thursday, May 11

Today was a sort of blah, of sorts.
I drank up water by the quarts,
Head was red, ears were warm,
Guess, for my case, that's the norm.

Friends and family call, concerned.
A care-receiver role is what I have earned.
Sweet Sue is watching my every move.
Whatever I do, she must approve.

If I act sick, I get more care
So I sit there blah in my comfy chair
And Sue responds with her gentle heart.
Don't know what I'd do without her. She's smart.

Friday, May 12

Mildly blah but few hiccups today.
Happy the itching's almost gone away.
Still burning throat and warmish glow
But wish other parts would decide to 'go'.

I'm told to take one day at a time,
That this could be a longish climb
Or at least a new journey, so get a good grip
Now how can we make this a happier trip?

With a bundle of pills hanging down by my side
I'll try to keep joking and take it in stride.
If I fall off the wagon and have a surprise,
I'll know Sue is there to help me arise.

Saturday, May 13

Still feeling queasy, told to stay
Away from public crowds – today
So skipped the Mended Hearts big meeting –
'Cuz I don't need what they are eating.

But I missed their planned election.
Hope they go in the right direction.
I've tried hard for last four years.
Now it's up to all my peers.

So today I just stayed home,
Put away my old black comb.
Figured I'll not need it soon
Though hair's still here on this baboon.

REFLECTIONS ON WEEK 1

One week down, a lifetime to go
New challenge, 'nother test.
With immune system down, It'll be a new show,
I'm sure I'll come out best.

They say the worst is yet to come,
I'll feel more lethargy
But I learned at Bennett years ago
"The best is yet to be".

So traveling Cancer Lane again
With prostate seeds 'behind me'
And twenty years of heart disease
Leaves plenty to remind me

To keep your chin up, be a pin-up,
Sing your favorite song,
Get your exercise, eat right,
The 'rest' will come along.

WEEK 2

Sunday, May 14 (Mother's Day)

Getting tough to just 'sleep tight',
Edgy, tossing, turned all night.
Feet got cold so socks on right,
Bathroom visits - - - -typical night!

Need more Colace than a smidgen.
(Great to have a stool pigeon.)
Eating slower, voice is changing,
Guess the body's rearranging.

Mother's Day, so lunch at Dan's,
Happy family – lots of plans.
Grand girls busy, tons of babble,
Home to beat sweet Sue at Scrabble.

Monday, May 15

A turtle sat upon my chest
Most of the morning, I suggest.
So off to Dr. C we flew.
He said "That's typical for you.

Try some Maalox as you need it,
You will live, Bill, as I read it".
So rest I took – and yes, more pills
But still feel minor blahs and chills.

Sue was worried, bless her heart,
Caring for me is still her art.
Cards and phone calls coming in-
Such a journey we begin.

Tuesday, May 16

Settling in 'tween 'blah' and 'crappy',
Walk around but daily nappy.
Pills for this and pills for that,
Pills for when I just feel flat.

Mild dizzy spells – a few.
(My kids would say that's nothing new.)
Sleeping better in the night,
Eating's almost a delight.

Could wish for better knee and shoulder.
Is this the price for getting older?
And yet I'm walking and above ground,
Expect long time before I'm shoved down.

Wednesday, May 17

Again today I tried to smile
Sue says that that's my favorite style.
In spite of body 'yucks' so weird
The worst of warnings ain't appeared.

So drive I did, took Sue out shopping
For things like that, she has not stopping.
We got the milk, bananas, too
At the store – where our lunch was a zoo.

With friends who care and ailments share,
It is a feeling beyond compare.
Many say they pray for us.
I guess I'm causing quite a fuss.

Thursday, May 18

Blobs in stomach, throat and head
Let me know that I'm not dead.
So I get out, driving, moving
Though the body's not approving.

Cold hands and feet I try to ignore
'Cuz, what the heck, had that before.
Before this glorious disease took hold
To sometimes make me feel more old.

But we know friends who are worse off,
Who also fight to keep the hearse off.
Seems everyone has something wrong
So pick your challenge, sing your song.

Friday, May 19

Generally, I'm feeling better,
Since it's cold, I wear a sweater
And a jacket and a hat.
Keeping warm is where I'm at.

Breakfast out with guys from church,
Helpful info's what I search.
Of course, they all have their own problems,
Mental, physical, other goblins.

Heard 'bout others deathly sick
So staying alive is still my trick.
Wish everyone who feels strife
Were fortunate as I – with WIFE!

Saturday, May 20

The refrigerator light is very, very bright
When it's the only light in the middle of the night
And the light above the oven, needing just a little shovin'
Led me to the grahams and milk – that I was lovin'.

That helped settle down my tummy,
I felt so very like a dummy.
  But there I was at two,
  Milk and crackers did I chew,
Back to bed, no longer feeling quite so crumby.

But today was very good, feeling better than I should
Hoping every day I would, be as upbeat as I could.
Even breakfast out with ladies (was the Grief
  Group from the church),
Found that helping other people keeps me up on top my perch.

REFLECTIONS ON WEEK 2

Another week of readjustment
Getting advice sublime:
As the roads and time go by,
"Take one day at a time".

Trouble doesn't get us down,
It's just another path,
Another challenge, another clown,
Another time to laugh.

I've still got knee and shoulder troubles,
Itching's coming back.
Full speed ahead to face these bubbles
While being a 'cardiac'.

Advice we've handed out this week
To family and a friend:
"Change is constant, be strong — not weak,
I hope you comprehend."

WEEK 3

Sunday, May 21, 2006

Feeling good again today
So went to church and went to pray.
So many people doing same
To help me on is their kind aim.

The weather's cold and windy, wet
So I'll not walk the block just yet.
I (wrongly) search for such excuses
And save them up for other uses.

Our dinner was chilly – no, chili — con carne,
Greatest meal all day, by darny.
Still am drinking lots of water.
Just 'cuz it's the thing I oughter.

Monday, May 22

Skipped another evening meeting,
Person there is sneezing, bleating.
Shaving less, the beard's not growing
But guess what's coming next? or going!

Back to normal taste and plumbing,
Can hardly wait to see what's coming.
Not much loss of weight or pep,
Feel quite lucky – but it's just first step.

I don't sit around feeling up a tree.
Crazy me – I'll write poetry.
Keeps old brain cells occupied
So mind won't take a wide stride ride.

Tuesday, May 23

Another turn in the road of life,
Watching for signals is a job of sweet wife.
Turn down Essjay, says my proctor,
Here to see another doctor.

Dr. N. H., a nice neurologist
Examined my shoulder, then turned with a twist,
"The biopsy probably damaged a nerve,
It'll heal in time, we'll just observe".

Along with my knee, this was a bummer –
Must give up my tennis, at least for the summer.
Oh well, onward, other things
To keep me busy; see what brings.

Wednesday, May 24

The weather is warmer, went out to buy plants,
Gotta keep moving, get off of my......pants,
Then we visited Mike, old Jaycee and great guy,
A medical miracle, much sicker than I.

It's good to feel good, as I'd hoped that I would,
I'm encouraged to keep laughing, as always I could.
Taking no extra pills does give me thrills
It hardly feels like I have any ills.

Oh, last night when Sue was out at church meeting
And I was left home to do my own eating,
I fixed my hot dog, but mistook the ketchup,
Used similar bottle – was French dressing – wretch-up!!

Thursday, May 25

We started the day out Orchard Park way,
Seeing Dr. Lou Edda who proceeded to spray-
Was it nitrogen freezing some spots on my head?
"Precancerous keratoses" I think is what she said.

Dermatologists are thorough, she checked all my skin,
Gave me cream for what itches and hope that I'll win.
Then in afternoon and evening, Sue worked with one aim:
Write short biography of Dad for his Tennis Hall of Fame.

Yes, I finally broke down and shaved off a fuzzy beard.
I detect slowing of the growing, though it sure feels weird.
So the day was busy/dizzy though I did get in a nap.
That and healthy eating keep me from the fat cat trap.

Friday, May 26

'Twas a dark and dreary day today,
A drizzly rain but warm display.
Get my spirits down? Heck, no,
Just glad I'm not six feet below.

The grass is growing, firming up,
Baby robins worming up.
Dinner: fish fry! Had the urge.
Once in a while, you have to splurge.

Saturday, May 27

Up in the morning, out in the yard,
Sue was the planter, I'll be the bard.
Flowers she potted all over the place,
I pretended to help her, stood by. Just in case.

Feels good to be able to move and to work
Though I didn't do too much – hey, I'm no jerk.
Twice I was able to take a nice nap,
Pretending to be sick – hey, I'm no sap.

REFLECTIONS ON WEEK 3

This week the journey went quite well,
The road ahead quite clear
Advice I got from friends, however
Is "Stick that in your ear.

"You never know what's down the road
But that keeps life exciting".
Each day I thank my God above
For help in cancer fighting.

Occasionally I hear from Jack,
My brother, I can tell.
He asks "You're always doing good
But are you doing well?"

I say "Thanks, Jack, I'm feeling fine,
Friends think I'm really sick"
Sue still watches every move.
I TRUST WE'LL LICK THIS QUICK.

WEEK 4

Sunday, May 28, 2006

End or beginning of another great week,
Feeling still good, in my funny physique.
So cleaned the garage, first sweeping, then hosing,
Worked hard enough to deserve afternoon dozing.

Sue spent the hot day planting and clipping,
Ripping and snipping, not slipping but dripping.
Flowers were delivered from church to sick me,
A thoughtful donation, a kind remedy.

Monday, May 29

This is Memorial Day, a time to reflect
On the sacrifices made by those we respect:
Our military service folk who died in past wars
For freedoms to enjoy – both for mine and for yours.

For lunch, off to Canada, to see an art show
Of friend, Dr. Bob, who had quite a glow
As his paintings were hung around chimneys with care
In hopes of lotsa people to buy them right there.

Tuesday, May 30

Still feeling well, another day, I repeat
And we set a new record for May 30 heat.
Hit 90 degrees, so Sue just hosed flowers,
Got out the fans to help pass the hours.

This morning, a visit to Dr. C. we went,
The usual pre-check-up to infusion event.
He was happy to see the neck lump disappeared
But also is going: the growth of weird beard.

Wednesday, May 31

Last night, about three, I staggered out to the kitchen
For crackers and peanut butter I had been itchin'
But morning was better – met friends for breakfast
Buckwheat pancakes and syrup - make me sound reckless??

The afternoon - watching Sue shopping for shoes,
The evening – watching dumb television news.
Right now, the road ahead seems pretty clear
But I gotta stay alert for what will appear.

Thursday, June 1

"I'm losing it, I'm losing it," I cried from my bed
Oh, it's only the hair on the top of my head.
It suddenly started to fall out last night.
I'm beginning to look like the funniest sight.

It seems hair is falling right out of the sky.
Sue started laughing, I could just cry.
There wasn't much before, there's even less now.
To dear Mother Nature I have to kowtow.

Friday, June 2

Out for breakfast with the boys,
Shared our problems and our joys.
Evening out with monthly bridge group.
By bedtime, it all made me droop.

Tiny hairs upon my pillow –
I almost weep just like the willow.
But I won't waste time or even pout,
Recalling what I've lived without it.

Saturday , June 3

Keeping busy, getting out,
Koinonians for breakfast, first Saturday, no doubt.
Lunch and walking mall with Sue,
ATM, then home we flew.

Afternoon again for rest,
Evening out to friends – the best.
Feeling good and feeling able,
Like a horse's home -– I am quite stable.

REFLECTIONS ON WEEK 4

Down the road, another week,
It's not been hard to bear.
The principal visable sign of change —
The leaving of my hair.

I've written poems of thanks and hope
To American Heart and Watercise.
A lot of people seem to care
And want to sympathize.

I don't think that I look real sick
(Though lost about four pounds)
But Sue keeps saying that I am
And gives me smiles — and frowns.

So what is coming up next week?
Infusion — second set.
Let's get on and through with it
And just forget to fret.

WEEK 5

Sunday, June 4, 2006

In church today, I thanked them for prayers
And said 'I was losing it – but only my hairs.'
They showed their love and honest concern.
Friends do care, I again did learn.

This afternoon, I slept three hours,
Then woke up fast, to smell the flowers.
Trimmed some trees out front so they'll
Help get sweet Sue off my tail.

Monday, June 5

Set of chemos number two
Began today and the time? It flew.
Even slept through some of the dripping.
(My alertness must be slipping).

No side effects showed up today
But ready still for come-what-may.
Meanwhile <u>Water</u> am I drinking!
Gotta stay loose is what I'm thinking.

Tuesday, June 6

Back to Dr. "C"'s Medical Group
To get more chemo and blood-work scoop.
Jaycee Jim kindly took me home
Great to have a friend (and HE carries a comb).

Friends told me today that if that's all I get,
I'd better not fret, but be happy! You bet.
Am hoping tonight I sleep better than last.
It didn't go fast. I'm so glad that it's passed.

Wednesday, June 7

Slept quite well, I must admit.
(Only wet my pajamas a bit).
The nuisance was hiccups, on and off all day long.
My tastebuds went weak – but I try to be strong.

Feel quite well for Day Three and the shot
For what I expected for what I have got.
So I kept myself busy doing Mended Hearts stuff
For the Saturday Banquet and my talk off the cuff.

Thursday, June 8

Not too bad for the "day after three",
Still better than I expected it to be.
Minor throat burnings and occasional 'hics'
But a pill here and there seemed to be the right fix.

Did shopping, some gardening and just keeping busy
And fortunately, no spells that I could call dizzy.
A super meal Sue fixed for dinner:
Fried potatoes and meatloaf and cantaloupe – a winner!

Friday, June 9

Waves of heartburn flow and go,
Wish other systems would do so.
Still perceiving hair still leaving,
Now believing but not grieving.

Face is flushing, seems I'm blushing,
Time goes slow, wish it were rushing.
What comes next and what do we know?
--JUST ANOTHER DAY AFTER CHEMO!

Saturday, June 10

Had to MC the Mended Hearts Luncheon
And give awards – a biennial function.
New national president, Margaret, spoke,
She installed two of four officers – and that's no joke.

But our local chapter will survive
As long as I can stay alive.
Four hours on tip-toe got me tired
But as president - I'm retired, not fired.

REFLECTIONS ON WEEK 5

Another journey week gone by,
It's over and I'm glad.
Compared to just four weeks ago
Was better than I had.

So things continue looking up,
More hopeful down the road.
In spite of knee pain, burning throat,
I'm not on overload.

Just taking it easy, one day at a time
Is what I'm trying to do.
Seems to be easier all the time
Because I have my Sue.

WEEK 6

Sunday, June 11, 2006

Attended church, lunch out today,
Slept the afternoon away.
I'd guess you'd say the blahs are back.
Getting well? Just down the track!

Still waves of throat-burn/irritation
Passing headaches, warm head sensation.
It's up and down like a bouncing ball
But can't complain much overall.

Monday, June 12

They were right! I was not happy.
Last night, got there! I felt 'crappy'.
Doctor, nurses – heaven forbid,
Promised I'd make it – and I did.

Didn't feel like doing a thing
In my Castle, I'm not king.
Slept this afternoon and evening,
What the heck am I achieving?

Sue still doing all the gardening,
Digging weeds with muscles hardening.
She checks on me, asks questions deeper.
Again, I know, <u>I sure will keep her!</u>

Tuesday, June 13

Toes are freezing, hands are cold –
(Couldn't be I'm getting old).
Head gets warm, throat gets rough.
Hey, this lymphoma stuff is tough.

Knee is throbbing, I'm near sobbing
From my upbeat mode – it's robbing.
But I'll hang in there, day by day
Knowing this too goes away!

Wednesday, June 14

This is Flag Day, June fourteen
But I'm not flying, I'm in between
The sappy days that I just had
And 'little better', for which I'm glad.

I watched Sue garden like a trooper,
She's amazing, she is super.
Gives me best of food and drink.
She surely wants me 'in the pink'.

Thursday, June 15

Another night of little sleep,
Tried again to count those sheep.
Nothing worked – not milk or grahams
So slept in daytime – like the lambs.

Carpet cleaned and Hannas come visit,
Sue's car check-up. What day is it?
After dinner, a block party –
Kept my mind alert and hearty.

Friday, June 16

Same three pit stops every night
Assure me things are going right.
Slower getting better this time.
Trying to behave on this climb.

Three friends came to us this day
With problems greater than <u>my</u> resume'.
Lifelong depression, heart attack,
Massive stroke – a left side whack.

Makes my problems seem so small
When others go and hit the wall.
Support and comfort we will give
Through these challenges, we will live.

Saturday, June 17

Still have blahs; I drink and rest,
The weather's hot, I'm overdressed.
Some itching's back on shoulders, chest
Dry mouth, too, but feeling blessed.

Glad I'm not at all depressed
Or even feeling slightly stressed.
I continue to be impressed
About my Sue – she is the BEST.

REFLECTIONS ON WEEK 6

Six gone, twenty to go
Weeks are counting down.
I'm vertical, above the ground
'Bout that I cannot frown.

Friends with problems worse than ours
Breaks my heart to hear 'em
But I listen to their stories,
Do not fear 'em; hear 'em.

Life is difficult! Face the fact
For all — it's universal.
So get up and move, find your own groove
This ain't no dress rehearsal.

WEEK 7

Sunday, June 18, 2006

Another hot and humid one-
To church and home but out of the sun.
Dan and E.A gang came in –
Father's Day picnic with our kin.

As on most of Sunday nights,
Dave usually calls with his hi-lights.
I'm feeling better (except for knee),
A restful day with family.

Monday, June 19, 2006

Felt quite normal all day long,
Hardly feel there's anything wrong.
Didn't even take a nap –
Not too bad for this old chap.

Even took a walk a bit,
Gotta do much more of it.
Gotta lotta things to do.
Where's the energy? It flew.

Tuesday, June 20, 2006

The day went fine until dinner time
When the tragic news came to light:
My friend and partner – 30 years,
Don Litwin, died last night.

His brother told me when I called
To ask how Don was doing.
I guess a second stroke came on
Which was his last undoing.

His wife and daughters must be in shock,
They had no sign or warning.
I sure will miss my trusted friend,
I'm sure we'll long be mourning.

Wednesday, June 21, 2006

Today it hit: TWO friends who died.
Almost left me google-eyed.
A former pastor, Lew S. Brown-
Four years of cancer wore him down.

The other, Don Litwin, from massive stroke
Died in four days – never awoke.
So suddenly gone, no preparation,
Bewildered family, no explanation.

A friend from Jaycees – 50 years
Can't help but bring a man to tears.
Life's so fragile, need I say?
Obviously, this crashed my day.

Thursday, June 22, 2006

From the news I still am reeling,
Thankful that I still have feeling.
I sometimes wonder why I'm still here.
There is a purpose – so get in gear!

I appreciate each hour and minute.
Today – feel good, glad I'm in it.
Tired often, itching still.
Compared to others, I'm not ill.

Friday, June 23, 2006

This morning, a memorial service for Don.
Hundreds showed up, who will try to carry on.
He served his church and community well
As a "gentleman", he did excel.

A luncheon followed, a time to grieve,
Then home to bed, my rest to retrieve.
I thank the Lord for sparing me
For further work in ministry.

Saturday, June 24, 2006

Church's Grief Group met to eat,
A monthly feat, an upbeat treat.
Widows come; we try to grin.
With the week I had, I fit right in.

Otherwise, the day was plain,
Didn't have to use my brain –
That seems to be on permanent wane
But I'm alive so won't complain.

REFLECTIONS ON WEEK 7

Feeling pretty good this week
Except for deaths of friends.
'Tis said that's part of life and I'm
Getting use to the message it sends.

I try to appreciate every day
And cheer up other folk
And thank my God I'm still around
And able to poke a joke.

Every road has bumps and detours,
Potholes, stop signs, spills
But I'll keep driving, steering, smiling
'Til I'm really 'over the hills'.

WEEK 8

Sunday, June 25, 2006

Hard to believe it was twenty years
Ago today that I changed gears,
Got five new grafts around my heart
And healthier living got a start.

I dreamt of big day celebrated
But quiet home rest's all it rated.
Church folk thought I'm doing well
Just 'cuz I said "I'm feeling swell".

Can I go another twenty?
Think not. Maybe ten is plenty.
Meanwhile, drink my water, rest,
Enjoy Sue's cooking, it's the best.

Monday, June 26, 2006

A cloudy, muggy normal day.
Tired but fine – that seems the way.
Fourth week after infusion stuff –
Still don't feel I have it rough.

Tuesday, June 27, 2006

A warmish day of clouds and rain
But in the bod, just one small pain:
When lying down, my knee does bawl.
(Perhaps I shouldn't rest at all.)

So up I get and check my hair
And soon forget the pain was there.
Also gone or disappearing:
The hairs on top, few persevering!

Wednesday, June 28, 2006

Tired. Tired. Tired. Tired.
If I were employed, I'd be fired.
Loafed but laddered up, cleaned gutter,
Took a short walk; 'tired', I utter.

Thursday, June 29, 2006

Tired still, I do repeat,
Layed on the bed or slept on my seat.
Watched Sue pack our suitcase full –
She's wonderful, that ain't no bull.

Friday, June 30, 2006

From the town of Tonawanda and the Falls of old Niagara,
Drove we east to visit Murphys in the town of Canandaigua.
Toured the Culinary Center, a brand new piece of culture
Featuring wines of New York State and our famous agriculture.

In the evening took an Art Walk through the streets
  of their downtown,
Had a good time with the Murphys – cuz with them,
  you just can't frown.
With warm winds through the bedroom, we slept "well,"
  to be precise.
In spite of being surrounded by a thousand Mickey Mice.

Saturday, July 1, 2006

Lazy rising in the; morning, starts with
  Mother Murphy's oatmeal.
Gotta be a good day: fresh air is what you feel.
Drove with Richard to the dump to unload their weekly trash
While Sue and Carol shopped (spending
  all our hard-earned cash).

Early afternoon watch tennis – Wimbledon thrills,
Then got the two-dollar tour past Sandi and Phil's
New house and big farmland, passed fish ponds and all.
This Finger Lakes area is starting to sprawl.

Good meals the chef serves here, and good conversation –
Went into the night for amplification.
The knee needed consideration but not medication
But I still feel 'super' – as a generalization.

REFLECTIONS ON WEEK 8

I'm seeing more clearly where this journey is leading –
This road with its hilltops and valleys –
To self-understanding and pleading and reading
That helps me drive safely through alleys.

I'm reminded again "Accept life as difficult",
That I'm wrong to think life should be easy,
That I have to face my problems and pains
And solve them without acting queasy.

WEEK 9

Sunday, July 2, 2006

Back from Murphys' two-night stay,
Had a good time as get-away.
Dashed back home, we dare not shirk
As I watch Sue do all the work.

Neighbors in for mid-day snack.
They're good to us, can't pay them back.
So tired we got, and the weather was hot,
For a holiday weekend, it's just the right spot.

Monday, July 3

July infusion starts Series three,
Another day toward "Big L" victory.
Three hours chemo drip but I feel no sign.
The Doc said blood count "was just fine".

Lunch on way home, then two hour nap,
Feeling good, too: the right kneecap.
So half way through my chemo treatments!
Weight? Down a bit, but I love my eat-ments.

Tuesday, July 4

Independence Day, of course.
Free day between the chemo's force.
Still feel so well, no aches or pains
And I feel I'm making cancer gains.

A quiet day, just Sue and me,
Our own little happy family.
Starting to think of 'sizing down',
Visited friends who've moved around.

Wednesday, July 5

Back to CHOP-shop infusion of stuff.
Funny – I'm feeling still up to snuff.
Hardly any side effect
So not feeling like a wreck.
Did sleep well this afternoon,
Gotta keep up my "immune".

Mended Hearts group met tonight
To spread the light upon their plight.
Since I'm no long president,
To spread the work is their intent.
Soon they'll be learning all I did,
The many jobs I'm glad I'm 'rid'.

Thursday, July 6

Heavenly hiccups to have and to hold,
They come and they go and they come – they're so bold.
They keep me from sleeping – and waking, for that matter.
Along with burning throats: get them off of my platter.

Friday, July 7

Today, it was different, I started to slack,
Slowed down to look at the whole body pack.
Hairs are depleting on head, legs and arms.
Heavens, I'm loosing my fuzzy ole charms.

I'm loosing it too, in the energy field
To a summer of tennis I'm having to yield.
It's the thrashing in throat that 'yucks' me today
But knowing 'things pass', it will go away.

Saturday, July 8

With blahs coming back and my oomph gone astray,
Watching Winbledon tennis sure helps pass the day,
Dreaming I was there, to watch (and to play??) –
Just one of those wishes I'll have to delay.

The pain in the knee continues to be
The dominant bother that's bothering me.
Tylenol taken but no help is it makin',
Still, being unshaken, I'll go with the aichin'.

REFLECTIONS ON MONDAY'S VISIT TO THE ONCOLOGIST

(Composed at 2:25 am on July 4ᵗʰ)

I asked Dr."C" about shooting the knee.
He would say, "It's OK, if you have to ask me".
Since that very hour, that knee has felt better.
Do you think the knee's scared, thinking I'm a go-getter?

That I'll run for a gun just to fix the dumb thing?
Well, that's an idea — might end the small sting.
First I'd check with that doctor, of my joints, of course.
I know he's shot knees and hips (maybe a horse).

No, I'll just wait and see and hope for the best
That the knee stays pain-free and gives me some rest.
So should I go walking and give it a test?
Or wait for the spirit to move me, unstressed?
Stay tuned for the answer, it may come in jest.
For now, I am feeling I surely am blessed!

WEEK 10

Sunday, July 9, 2006

Skipped church 'cuz I'm lazy, watched tennis instead.
The afternoon 'wasted' on comfortable bed.
Lunched with Dan and the family, communication to revamp,
Libby off to Germany, Maggie–soccer camp.

Feel I'm headed toward "crappy", at that I'm not happy.
My throat and red head make me go take a nappy.
The warm face and neck remind me of what I've got
And the truth is the warmness is really not so hot.

The throat waves occasionally bother or burn.
I take 'em in turn, just a minor concern.
The itching's been gone for more than a week.
The shoulder still drooping – makes strange physique.

Monday, July 10

Taste in mouth again diminished,
Seems more than a week – the itching's finished.
Tired, though – just bop around
Looking like a haggard hound.

With bugs on bushes, weeds arising,
Garage wall peeling (not surprising),
Rooms need painting I'm despising –
We talk more about down-sizing.

Tuesday, July 11

Tired again the whole day through,
But lots of odd jobs did I do.
Sue was gone to a presbytery meeting,
Lunch alone, but at least, I'm eating.

Alan Dibbard starting scrapping
Garage wall peeling that I'm escaping.
Sue out again for bridge tonight
And still my throat is not quite right.

Wednesday, July 12

OK, OK, I've had enough!
My stupid esophagus just ain't up to snuff.
Some minor pains in head and knee
That come a while and then they flee.

I guess this comes with "the week that's after"
But it sure has modified my laughter.
Today we had a lot or rain –
Could that be causing "humidity pain"?

Thursday, July 13

Well, today, the weather got hot;
Was I feeling better? Not!
Sue says I look like soup left over.
At least I'm not <u>below</u> the clover.

Met with investment man, Tom Lunt.
"Your things look good", he said up front.
I wonder where he looked for that
'Cuz inside me, I feel like 'splat'.

Still getting calls and visits from friends-
'Twould be heaven if that never ends.
Meanwhile, rest and water drink,
Down the road, I'll feel more pink.

Friday, July 14

Five per cent better today than before
But that's not saying much 'cuz I'm keeping score.
Voice is still weak (like the brain up above it)
But food's tasting better. It had better – 'cuz I love it.

Went shopping for food, ended up with five pants-
Summer clearance we came on by chance.
More really hot weather with humidity high,
It's tough to stay cool but us 'cool cats' still try.

Saturday, July 15

Warm, humid neighborhood walk,
Knee held up so I can't squawk.
Throat seems better, taster too.
Made it through my green tea brew.

Started cleaning up the basement,
Tossing junk that needs displacement.
Sue found old things that aren't worthwhile
(Almost put <u>me</u> in same pile).

Dinner our with Ruby and Ray-
(Cost an arm, two legs to pay)
But it was pleasant, cool and nice;
We listened lots, exchanged advice.

REFLECTIONS ON WEEK 10

I guess this week I had no 'Reflections'

Another example of my imperfections.

WEEK 11

Sunday, July 16, 2006

Wow, I got another five per cent
Better as the day was spent.
Rested some and worked down cellar,
It's cooler there, as a basement dweller.

Never wore my socks all day –
Barefoot boy with guts of clay.
Mostly didn't wear a shirt.
Felt damn good, to be quite curt.

More damn itching around the shoulders,
Those lumpy red spots are getting bolder
(Like ants in our kitchen, invading the place,
The carpenter type we're also trying to erase).

Monday, July 17

Another scorching, muggy day,
We kept the fans all turned to 'play'.
Drinking Gatorade and juices
By the bottle – no excuses.

Lunch with Jaycees, ant spray shopping-
They're advancing, Aunt Sue wants stopping.
Baking soda, scour the kitchen,
Stomp them dead – while I go itching.

Trying Benadryl for itch,
Looks like hives, makes shoulders twitch.
Just another hoop to jump,
Just another in-the-road bump.

Tuesday, July 18

Another day and even hotter
Made me feel like a worn-out blotter
So tired I was, so rest I did-
I guess I ain't no teen-age kid.

Knee not hurting, mouth still dry-
A strange, ole body I can't deny.
Switch my case with others? Never!
'Cuz I've got the best wife ever!

Wednesday, July 19

My thoughts and feelings are the same
That yesterday's two verses proclaim.
So why should I exert myself
And take my brains down off the shelf?

Thursday, July 20

We were 'bed and breakfast' for Murphy's last night
Between their dinner and luncheon invites.
Out early in morning for semi-annual check-up
By Dr. Vantini re joints, <u>not</u> from neck-up.

The hip he found hip, just needs to be watched.
The knee, on the other hand, is still slightly botched.
No shot and no surgery, 'keep active and moving'
Do water aerobics, of that, he's approving.

Then lunch with Jack Mimmack, my old tennis friend,
We shared family stories and laughed to the end.
In Mid-afternoon, drove Kenny to be tested
At Literacy Volunteers, then I'm home to be rested.

Even filled up the gas tank – it's 'gas sale' day.
Saved five cents a gallon (I get carried away).

Friday, July 21

Start with Mens' Breakfast and Family Tree food,
Three of us made it – we talked and we chewed.
Sue finally bought sneakers for comfort and walking,
Now her 'soul' will be happy whenever she's talking.

The body feels better, I think I'm alive,
Kept drinking my liquids to thrive and survive.
Itching's 'bout gone, as long as I don't touch,
The weather's too muggy, we don't eat too much.

Saturday, July 22

Cool and gray but a comfortable day,
Breakfast with Grief Group – we all had our say.
Sue did the shopping, I goofed away,
Keep feeling better – can only say 'yea'.

REFLECTIONS ON WEEK 11

As my journey continues through life and lymphoma,
And the road is lined with learning,
I'm beginning to realize I don't have control
Over some of the directions we're turning.

I didn't seek cancer or joints that would hurt
Yet I won a couple of each
But greater than those are the blessings received —
Of family and love I could preach.

I'll control what I can and accept what I can't
As God continues to drive,
I'm a passenger now, so enjoying the ride
To 'somewhere', we'll safely arrive.

WEEK 12

Sunday, July 23, 2006

Made it to church but after-noon: slept,
Watched Sue dig some weeds, then her mess I up-swept.
Generally feeling good, minor itching returning,
Should be a great week – for which I am yearning.

Monday, July 24

Another good day, as I walked in the mall,
Had a visit from Ralph – just a one-hour call.
My legs sat in sunlight, a slight burn did they get;
My skin still is sensitive – how can I forget?
Good rest did I have in the mid-afternoon.
Gotta get better – sure hope it is soon.

Tuesday, July 25

Sue to eye Doc, then got hair cut.
We took Joan and JoAnn Litwin out – for what?
For lunch at the Roycroft, to hear their plights.
Packed for get-away, next two nights.

Wed-Thu-Fri, July 26, 27, 28

For the next three days (but just two nights),
Four couples gathered to see the sights
In Canandaigua, of all places renown,
To renew old friendships and see the town.

We drove the Dewitz's, meeting Bunny and Fred Drews,
Then John and Jeanne Aiken arrived from Syra – cuze.
Most of us were birds of a feather,
Attended elementary and high school together.

In the same Youth Group were seven of the eight
At University Church –so we celebrate.
But most distinct, it now appears:
We've all been married over fifty years!

So gather we did at Motel Super Eight
And walked the waterfront after we ate.
Back for our naps; too warm for coat,
And a sunset cruise on a paddlewheel boat.

(Cont'd)

Thursday – the Wine and Culinary Center,
New tourist attraction and a freebee to enter.
New York agriculture and wines they promote,
We stayed for light lunch and treated our throat.

Then we perused the shops along Main Street,
Tired were our feet so more nap and then eat.
The Inn on the Lake was the fancy dinner place
(Though some felt the food didn't keep up the pace).

Friday after breakfast we all did depart
To gather next year – if we're healthy and smart.
My body held up for the 200 miles
But Sue's started creaking – made it hard on the smiles.

Saturday, July 29

Day of napping and of resting,
Trimming bushes, lunch digesting.
Three o'clock at church was hot:
Ben and Alexa tied the knot.

Fans helped out to keep us cool,
Drinking water is the rule.
What I lack is energy,
I guess I'm just a casualty.

MY NEGLECTION---

---NO TIME FOR REFLECTION

WEEK 13

Sunday, July 30, 2006

Sue has back pains, I am dragging
So we didn't make church 'cuz both were sagging.
Linda Hershey brought flowers – a thrill.
Guess the church still thinks I'm ill.

Tiredness best describes my condition
So in bed I rested – with my own permission.
Tomorrow rings the next infusion bell,
Sure hope it helps to get me well.

Monday, July 31

Finally, infusion set Number Four,
Three hours of dripping – and tomorrow: more.
The port is left in my arm overnight
In hopes that St. Nicholas – and cancer – take flight.

No effects felt just yet –but another heat wave
With temps in the 90's, I hafta behave.
Drink water, of course, but staying still as I can
And chasing humidity with our tool: the FAN!

Tuesday, August 1

Heavenly hiccups, they're starting in plenty,
One-two-three to five-ten-and-twenty.
A (hic) pain they are, a (hic) nuisance by far
It seems quite bizarre but for me (hic), it's par.

Otherwise feeling fine from the two-hour infusion.
Left arm says it's tired from so much intrusion.
Slept poorly last night, only up thrice.
If you don't have lymphoma: don't get it, not nice!

Wednesday, August 2

A mere shot today – oh, just in the arm
By a cute chemo nurse with plenty of charm.
This ends the fourth series – the lymphoma 'should' be gone.
A CAT scan due soon on this poor little pawn.

Those (hic) hiccups surround me from darkness 'til dawn,
They interrupt sleep when I'm tired – [pardon... y a w n].
Sometimes holding breath will make them go'way
Or drinking from far side of glass – what a day!

It also is hot – record heat and humidity.
(Pardon me while I go and check my liquidity.)
Sweet Sue has us living in much cooler basement –
Though no bed or bathroom,
  could get use to this displacement.

Thursday, August 3

Fourth series now over, what will they affect?
On the throat and the taster they have no respect
But bear it I will, I don't feel <u>too</u> ill.
Even feel that my energy is going UP hill.

Same hiccups today, come as one, three or eight
So I certainly don't want to overstate
The nuisance they are, 'cuz I still have a life
And a wonderful wife who is sharp as a knife.

Friday, August 4

Took Les to Men's Breakfast, had their Special (I cheat) –
Love that bacon and eggs and pancakes to eat.
'Course most of the time, I eat Sue's preparations:
Right-size and healthy, with improvisations.

Cooler today, more comfortable for walking.
The throat or the voice box – more scratchy for talking.

This week: start and finished a church-loaned book
By award-winner Joan Didion, on what really her shook:
Sudden death of a husband, then daughter, then grief,
A "Year of Mystical Thinking" and much disbelief.

Saturday, August 5

Another Family Tree Breakfast with six other guys
Trading stories, experiences (and maybe some lies).
Walked the block with my Suzie, enjoying the cool,
Still wishing the food would make me more drool.

From Thursday night meeting of some Mended Hearts,
We altered some duties and changed a few parts.
As newsletter editor, Sue offered to be.
(I'm sure that frustration will drive her up tree.)
A Steering Committee will run the whole show.
I'll just sit around and change gears to 'slow'.

REFLECTIONS ON WEEK 13

I'm half way through the whole procedure,
Time to take a peak
At how the body parts are feeling,
Where they speak or creak.

The toes are cold, night and day,
Left ankle — it's OK.
Right knee's behaving, feeling strong
As is the back — today.
Mouth is dry, but throat is better,
Dry hands start a-pealing.
Shoulder right is drooping still
But no pain am I feeling.

No hiccups but itching, red spots back,
Energy? Moderate at best.
All this makes me think I'm ill,
I'll go and take a rest.

WEEK 14

Sunday, August 6, 2006

Up for church and out for lunch
With the Hughes plus three – a bunch.
Weakness still in voice and throat.
(Weak in brain and you can quote.)

Picnic dinner at Dewitz's with flair,
Then Harry James concert in Clarence air.
It got me tired and feeling blah –
Something like an <u>old</u> grand-pa.

Monday, August 7

I made it! I made it! I finally got here:
The lousiest, crappiest Day of the Year!
Tuned me in to the Alma Mater
From Bennett High, as I got hotter:

> Hail to thee, o <u>Constipation</u>,
> Loud our voices raise,
> Ever will anticipation
> Sing for better days.

> Back in high school, all things possible,
> Everything seemed free,
> Now the road is blocked, impassable.
> Where's "the best is yet to be"?

> Hail to thee, o stool softener,
> Loud we sing our woe,
> Waiting, hoping it is oftener
> For all things to go.

Tuesday, August 8

Much better today than Monday was
'Cuz things got <u>going</u>, just becuz.
A little patience, a pill or two
Was all it took to help me through.

Perfect weather, liquids and rest,
Sue's great meals, I am so blessed.
Watched the Mens Doubles at the Racquet Club,
Hope to be back there, even as a sub.

Wednesday, August 9

Well, the blahs are still around,
Laziness, tiredness do abound.
Shoulders itching, feet feel frozen –
Not the comforts I'd have chosen.

Drink more water as mouth gets dry,
Chemo is great (I'll go and cry).
Weird is throat, weak is voice –
Learning and living is still my choice.

Thursday, August 10

Thrill of the summer: back on tennis court!
Played four games of doubles- the time it was short.
The guys were all gracious, they appreciate my try.
They said I did well (it's nice that they lie).

Voice still queasy, no singing operetta.
Shoulders still itching, so we saw Dr Lou Edda
She doesn't know the reason why
So biopsy next week – give it a try.

Friday, August 11, 2006

A few muscle aches, but it sure felt good,
Last night on the tennis court, I knew I could.
Walked tonight along Niagara River,
Cooler weather almost made me shiver.

Still, cool toes and hands and nose,
That's just the way my chemo goes.
Also keeps me blah and listless.
Does that mean I'm making progress?

Saturday, August 12

Cool and comfortable all day.
At least the weather was that way.
As for me, still cool, still blah,
Not quite ready to shout "hurrah!"

Watched Sue working better and better
On Mended Hearts upcoming newsletter.
She'd also shop, she'd also rest –
I'll tell the world: She IS the best!

REFLECTIONS ON WEEK 14

Daily I gaze at the mirror before me,
Will the hair come back on my head
After October, November, December?
Will it be curly? Or red?

Whatever the case, I'll take it in stride,
Return to important things.
Like writing poems for various friends
and walking 'round the block evenings.

WEEK 15

Sunday, August 13, 2006

Feeling better, feeling stronger,
Come on, lymphoma, how much longer?
Gotta get thru two more sessions,
Done so far without depressions.

Generally loafed again today,
Skipped church this morning along the way.
Sat and watched the world go by
Made it easy for time to fly.

Monday, August 14

Food's beginning to taste 'lil better
As August weather gets cooler and wetter.
A Benadryl a day's keeping itching at bay
So "normal" I'm nearing; to that I say 'Yea'.

We're treating ourselves to all kinds of fruit
Delivered here Saturday – big basket of loot.
A wonderful gift from the Agents' Association,
Maybe they heard I'm in degeneration.

Tuesday, August 15

Feeling more normal – it almost feels good.
Figured I'd get here – well, hoped that I would.
Still watching Sue busy with *Pulsebeat* and church work.
Think it makes me feel guilty? Heck, no. I'm no jerk.

Dental cleaning and X-rays, watching spot on my gums,
A sensitive area that goes and it comes.
Dentist said that it could be a burn or a tumor
'Cuz when I bite apple – I ain't got no humor.

Wednesday, August 16

Had a treat today – I was the sole guy
At a 30-women luncheon at My Tomato Pie.
We're losing the instructor of our water aerobics class –
Ginny took another job so is leaving us. Alas!

They gave her gifts, I read my poem,
Kissed more women – now I'll know 'em.
At the Aquatic Center, a lot goes on
But today, I saw them – with their clothes <u>on</u>!!

This afternoon I had to nap
To get back energy and zap.
Hugging all those women got me excited
Then Sue reminded me: <u>WE</u>'RE united.

Thursday, August 17

Back to the neurologist, Dr. N.H. by name,
Saw the shoulder still sloping and so did exclaim,
"It just may get better, on the other hand, it may not,
'Twill be a year to know either" – now figure out that plot.

Oh, happy again - I played six g-a-m-e-s of tennis
With three other decrepits – and I was no menace.
I had almost no strength and couldn't move my feet
But at least, I was out there – it was a neat treat.

Friday, August 18

As I arose, I heard myself say,
"I wonder what will happen today."
As it turned out, I continued to thrive,
Still love my dear wife, be glad I'm alive.

Had a biopsy done by my 'derm', Dr. Lou.
She stuck my right shoulder, said fondly "Adieu,
See you next week re the itching and cause".
Then patched me all up with band aids and gauze.

Then resting I did, to a nap I submit
While Sue did the gardening, the meals, the whole bit.
I did do the vacuuming, cleaned up from each meal
But wonder of wonders: Have I got a deal!

Saturday, August 19

Late breakfast today at the Family Tree.
The Grief Group from church: four ladies and me.
It was really all up-beat, we laughed and we talked.
Then after lunch, at "the Boulevard" I walked.

Sue did some shopping, then home where we napped,
Another exciting day and how we adapt.
Adapt to plugged ears, one stopped up with wax?
No! Rinse 'em and wash 'em, that's how Sue attacks.

REFLECTIONS ON WEEK 15

This week was much better, I felt almost human,
Tho generally more tired than I'd like.
Am I mastering the art of human decay?
Or should I just go 'take a hike'?

This summer is going and where have I gone?
Any progress, improvement to date?
This coming week should have test results
So I guess I'll patiently wait.

WEEK 16

Sunday, August 20, 2006

To church and pray. Another day.
Another day closer to hear what they say.
Is lymphoma still here? or am I now clear?
I hope they can tell me so I can go cheer.

The day was quite normal, felt good all the time.
Read paper, watched TV – the tennis was prime.
Got suitcases out – get ready for packing.
We leave in a week – don't want to be lacking.

Monday, August 21

This morning, a meeting for Adult Ed class.

[but I didn't write more, so I guess this will pass]

Tuesday, August 22

Big morning event – a full CT scan
Of pelvis and stomach and chest was the plan.
It's the second time since this stuff began.
I sure hope they find out that I'm spick – and – span.

They said I shouldn't have eaten for four hours prior
But took photos anyway – as was my desire.
Kathy, Lib and Maggie came here for dinner,
I ate more than they did – I'm not getting thinner.

Wednesday, August 23

I took Sweet Sue to her G-Y-N,
Then lunch with Joan in Orchard Park again.
To Session meeting in the evening
Feeling so good, I keep believing.

Thursday, August 24

I've waited all summer for this very day
When Dr. C called me, had this to say:
Said he to me, "The scans looked good.
The whatevers have shrunk, chemo did what it should.

"You still need more treatments, just two months for you".
That didn't excite me, for what I've been thru.
But I picked up myself, played 12 games of tennis,
Again, with the ancients who know I'm no menace.

Friday, August 25

This morning, I spoke to the Rehab group
At VA Hospital re Mended Hearts scoop.
Then saw Dr. Lou, she had a conclusion:
My shoulder itching was not a delusion.

It's Grover's Disease, sort of rare, it would seem
Topically treatable with cream (not ice cream).
She said it would take about six weeks to go.
I guess I can wait – everything seems slow.

Otherwise feeling reasonably well,
At feeling strong and peppy, I do not excel.

Saturday, August 26

Relaxing today, watched Sue do more packing,
She knows my strength and abilities are lacking.
She works so hard for me and us,
To get in her way is hazardous.

Suitcases out, clean clothes in,
Thinking of things other than my sensitive skin.
Monday we fly to Mended Hearts Convention
So 'straighten up, body' and pay attention.

REFLECTIONS ON WEEK 16

Well, this was the week that I've waited for,
The diagnosis should be back.
The cancer Doc said things looked good,
The skin Doc said she's on track.

Thank you, God, I'm glad to know
Our actions, thoughts and prayers
Have helped me get so far, so good —
In spite of losing hairs.

So Monday we are taking off
To Scottsdale for a week
Of Mended Hearts Convention there
As I'm feeling 'at my peak'.

WEEK 17

Sunday, August 27, 2006

I went to church while Suzie slept,
Came home and proved I was adept.
I printed out our Boarding Passes;
For my online skills, this sure surpasses.

Monday, Aug 28 – Saturday, Sept. 2

[There we were, way out West,
Met the test, it was the best!]

REFLECTIONS ON WEEK 17

No daily journal did I do
This 17th week of treatment.
Just took, we did, a real vacation
To see what real heat meant.

The entire week in Arizona
We laughed and learned a lot,
Met old friends from past conventions
But mostly, felt "the hot".

Mended hearts and caregivers all,
We had a busy time,
Tours and workshops, meals with Lackies,
I'm feeling in my prime.

Lots of walking, Southwest food,
We tended to get tired.
But overall, the week was great —
We got again inspired.

WEEK 18

Sunday, September 3, 2006

Up at four, leave Phoenix at nine,
Three hours of time change but feeling fine.
Home at six and unpack quick,
Company tomorrow for the dinner trick.

Dry mouth was my health complaint
For all last week, but now it ain't.
The only thing I feel more:
That I could sleep for days galore.

Monday, September 4

Laboring Day was what this was
'Til Twidles gave us a last-minute buzz.
"Traffic at Peace Bridge – one hour would lapse"
So canceled our dinner here and we got our naps.

Tuesday, September 5

Still feeling great, shoulder itching departs
But wouldn't you know it, INFUSION now starts.
Dr. C does assure us that progress is "good",
The last four months treatments have done what they should.

So let's start a fifth set today, to be sure:
Rituxin, etc, should help with the cure.
Three hours of infusion did not let me roam,
Sue dropped me off, Kirk Downing took me home.

Can't wait 'til tomorrow when more drugs appear,
Right now I feel fine, right now I could cheer.
The heparin port I have left in my arm
But keeping it straight so's to do it no harm.

Wednesday. September 6

Only two and a half hours of fusion delusion
While getting more drugs – which makes for confusion.
So today I asked questions to clear my thick head
Of what I am getting and what I have read.

Yesterday was RITUXAN to help make system immune.
Today started "CHOP' to get system attuned.
These all three today are to stop or slow growth
Of the darn cancer cells – I hope they do both.

C is for CYTOXAN – or Cyclo-phos-phomide.
H is for HY-DROXY-DOX-O-RUBICIN,
  which I took in stride.
O is for ON-COVIN, the brand name for Vincristine.
That was it today, but the future's to be seen.
P starts tomorrow (it's the poo that stopped today).
PREDNISONE – for "skin conditions"
  and whatever else they say.
So drugged I am, but feeling good.
Hiccups starting – 'like they should'.

Thursday, September 7

Third day drive to Dr. C's M-G (Medical Group)
For just a shot (and a two-dollar fee).
NEULASTA was this quick injection
To build white blood cells and fight infection.

Biggest effect from all this stuff
Is on-and-off hiccups, but it's not too rough
As I consider myself quite tough
(But hope I don't get nasty and gruff).

Kirk picked me up for dinner with Jaycees,
An old-time gang who always tease.
Steak I had though rarely done-
Rarely I eat it – so it was fun.

Friday, September 8

One of the worst, I must admit
(But not unbearable if you're fit).
All day long my head was hot,
Face as red as a burning pot.

Hiccups came and hiccups went,
Hot throat flashes were no accident.
A laxative here, a laxative there -
From top to bottom, still less hair.

Mild headache comes and goes,
What comes next, heaven knows.
Food beginning to taste like clay.
Other than that, 'twas a normal day!

Saturday, September 9

Much like yesterday, but gotta get thru it.
Have a Mended Hearts meeting, gotta just do it.
Itching is gone and my back feels strong,
Another day down as the journey goes along.

REFLECTIONS ON WEEK 18

Didn't take time for Reflections again.
If I don't shape up, I'll be sent to the pen.

WEEK 19

Sunday, September 10, 2006

I warm my cold hands on my red hot head
And appreciate the fact that I'm not yet dead.
At the other end (toes) – cold like my nose -
That could be left from my heart disease – who knows?

Anyway, got to church , then lunch in 'E. A.',
Met Anne, pronounced "on", for the school year to stay.
Eleventh grader from Germany, exchange student most sweet,
Libby's new friend who appears a neat treat.

Monday, September 11

Five years ago was the 9/11 attack,
We're somber today as all think back.
About 3000 innocents all lost their lives
From terrorist planes. And memory survives.

My body today, still feels attacked, too,
Cold and hot streaks, some joints to undo.
Not very comfortable so naps did I take.
Maybe feel better each time I awake.

Tuesday, September 12

Fifth day after shot and it would appear
Today's a competitor for "Worst of the Year".
Groggy – yes, crappy, I'm tired and weak.
So napping and resting and sleeping I seek.

Wobbly on feet so I try to keep moving,
Hugs from my Sweetie are always approving.
She fixes great meals that I try hard to eat.
She keeps me so healthy. She's great! I repeat.

Wednesday, September 13

Still a blah and yucky feeling,
Back to bed when I feel like reeling.
Ran some errands, then ran back home.
Safer here than out to roam.

Thursday, September 14

Need I say? Another day!
Crappy feeling – no go away.
Throat still blah, what can I say?
It was just: another day!

Not discouraged, not in sorrow
But have to think: 'Twill be better tomorrow.

Friday, September 15

Feeling 5% better than I yesterday was.
I wonder what <u>twenty</u> more days like this does!
Napping still feels good, so does scratching an itch.
Between the two pleasures, the better? is which?.

Saturday, September 16

Feeling 5% better than I yesterday was.
I wonder what <u>nineteen</u> more days like this does!
Napping still feels good, so does scratching an itch.
Between the two pleasures, the better? is which?.

REFLECTIONS ON WEEK 19

This journal's the lemonade from my lymphoma,
A drink that I didn't expect.
This journey is traveling thru Summer o-six,
A trip that I didn't elect.

With lemonade in hand and a trip well UNplanned,
We drove forward in faith and with hope.
Whatever's ahead, I shouldn't much dread
'cuz God won't let this dope mope.

WEEK 20

Sunday, September 17, 2006

People in church again said I "look good".
Have to wonder if they say what they think that they should.
But I take it with 'Thanks' and appreciate each plus,
Always hoping they're not just being felicitous.

My tongue feels like leather and I don't know whether
It's from chemo or hot soup or infection - even weather.
The whole mouth tastes funny, not making me sunny.
To say that I'm tasteless is right on the money.

This week coming up is the third after chemo.
If history repeats, we'll feel better – we know.

Monday, September 18

Well, heavenly days, the good Lord be praised.
Starting to feel human in most of the old ways.
Unfortunately, one old problem is back:
The itching on shoulders is about to attack.

I'll 'goo' it for now and take things at ease
Like Sue's new cell phone and lunch with Jaycees.
Dinner out, too, with Stephen Ministry group
And then back home – to bed and to droop.

Tuesday – Saturday,
September 19-20-21-22-23.

Whether napping or busy, time's gone by with a whiz,
Got lots of things done, don't e'en know what time it is.
These days have zipped by, hardly thinking of myself,
Meetings at church, busy as an elf.

REFLECTIONS ON WEEK 20

It went by so fast,
Seems like a blast.
Better than prior.
What a contrast!

WEEK 21

Sunday – Saturday,
September 24-25-26-27-28-29-30, 2006

24th: We lead Adult Class on "Gratitude, Then What?"
       And on to East Aurora for picnic we strut.
       We celebrate Libby's birthday sixteen.
       She's about to get permit – thinks it is keen.

25th: Semi-annual check-up with retiring Dr. Ordman
       He ordered more tests than would Norman, the Foreman.
       Helped Ken with his words for Literacy Volunteers.
       I'm still feeling great and having no fears.

26th: Minor shuffling of papers for ole Mended Hearts;
       Phone calls and reading, improving my smarts.

27th: Clearing the house for company coming.
       Steering meeting tonight to keep Mended Hearts humming.

28th: Jack and Lori pull in with their camper to stay
       For the weekend of family gathering - to play.
       Dave's in after midnight – we won't get much sleep.
       He's coming Jet Blue because it was cheap.

(Cont'd)

29th: Friday already and Murphys arrive,
Dinner for seven made Sue really strive.
Slides of the family and old recollections,
Sorted Dad's trophies and mused o'er reflections.

30th: Drove we all to Amherst Hills Tennis Center
Then Frank Lloyd Wright House did we enter.
Lunch from Andersons – beef on weck,
Little off the diet, but what the heck.

Carol Suess arrives and the Big Night just came:
Our Dad was inducted – the Buffalo Tennis Hall of Fame.
I accepted the plaque, gave 'Thank you' to all,
We chatted with old friends and just had a ball.

REFLECTIONS ON WEEK 21

Week went quickly, feeling great,
No time to think of self.
Now the journey looks so strait,
I put illness on the shelf.

WEEK 22

Sunday, Oct. 1, 2006

The Murphys slept upstairs and Dave in his slot,
Carol Suess – the den floor; five cars on the lot.
It's a once-in-a-lifetime reunion for us.
I'm still feeling well – for me, still a plus.

Jack, Lori and Dave joined for worship at church,
Then with Murphys we headed for Dan's East Aurora perch.
They invited more family – four Mossers, two Hosies,
'Twas a houseful of noises and picnic and cozies.

Then finally dispersing, we all went our ways,
Brought David back home and collapse on the chaise.

Monday, October 2

Up this morn at four o'clock,
Dave to airport – that's a shock.
Next to Med Group for more –
I think I've been this route before.

The journey revs up for one last time:
To see Dr. "C" and hope that I'm
Doing well to kill this thing –
Bring on Fall and make me sing!

Nine a. m., infusion started,
Noon-time to the door I darted.
Home to rest but feeling super,
To take last series like a trooper.

Tuesday, October 3

Back to Dr. "C"s Medical Group,
More infusion of the poop.
Sure hope this will be the last –
Now it seems the time's gone fast.

Still feel excellent, 'cept for a 'hic'.
So far today, I just can't kick.
Did get nap to keep so fine,
Then polished poem for Isabel's '99'.

Wednesday, October 4

Up early today for sounds of a sonogram,
Testing the aorta in the abdomen – I am.
Then off for my arm shot, to build up white cells-
The last of last series and said my 'farewells'.

The nurses were great, the cookies were fair,
The needles were many, they struck everywhere.
They treated me for cancer, not cardiac.
Nice as they were, I don't want to come back.

The hiccups keep coming but quickly do go
All by themselves – or I help with the flow.
Taste buds are slipping but otherwise 'I'm prime'
Feeling fit as a fiddle and sharp as a _____*.

* well, a nickel today.

Thursday, October 5

Not finished yet with doctors this week.
Downtown I drive for a Doppler test peek.
The carotids Maureen heard did well as they went:
"About the same as last time, zero and thirty percent".

Then back home to rest from my crazy disease
With hiccups now coming in ones, twos or threes.
No long series hiccups to test out some theories
But a strange throat developing which brings on the drearies.

Friday, October 6, 2006

Up early once more, men's breakfast at eight-thirty,
Get Les again and hope throat don't me hurty.
Walked 'round some blocks with Sue, my dependable,
Hoping from now on I'm getting more mendable.

Saturday, October 7

Still feeling weakfish, so skipped bridge last night
Today it was warmish so enjoyed the sun-light.
Puttered in garage, fall cleanup to start
While away at a Tea Party was my sweet Sweetheart.

As head still gets warm when esophagus screams,
A cold, wet bandana on top helps, it seems.
The Pack-attack of Nuisances more frequent today,
Could almost say 'crappy' is the way it would play.

REFLECTIONS ON WEEK 22

When my mind is keeping busy
And myself is on the move,
Then the pains of throat and body
Strangely seem to all improve.

So I guess the secret tells me
I should not lie down and rest.
Maybe keep on moving, grooving —
Could that really be the best?

I would think that I'd get tired
Wiggling, walking all day long.
Shall I call my doctor guru?
Will he tell me I am wrong?

Will he tell me what I need
Is BOTH to do the job?
Will he tell me if I don't
I'll just become a blob?

WEEK 23

Sunday, October 8, 2006

Coming days will be more happy
But for today: How do you spell 'Crappy'?
Didn't even get to church.
Sue went on, left me in lurch.

Knees are weak, mind is foggy,
Head gets warm, throat gets groggy.
Just a normal 'few days after'
Chemo drain; now where's the laughter?

Bathroom visits outscored naps.
Walk 'round block, then I collapse.
It makes me wonder, as I respond:
It's just like shopping: Bed, Bath and Beyond.

Monday, October 9

More of same, the blahs arrived
But I'm still lucky: I've survived.
Voice is waning, esophagus paining,
What a way for good health gaining!

Wedding anniversary fifty-two!
Wonderful years of life with Sue.
Out for breakfast, dinner, too.
That's the best that I could do!

Tuesday, October 10

Still feel blasted by chemo barrage
But moved patio furniture into garage.
Pulled tomato plants out of compost heap
And right away, boy could I sleep!

Really felt the exercise
All over the body, including the eyes.
Sue keeps saying: the Best is Rest
So I followed orders to my blanket nest.

Wednesday, October 11

Wobbly, wobbly, weak in knees,
Blahs still here – all of these.
Sue is slaving, cleaning clothes,
Me myself do nap, not prose.

Dr. O's letter said "Cholesterol high,
Get it down, give a try".
Change, change is the constant thing –
Wonder what winter and spring will bring.

Thursday, October 12

Ran some errands, packed some bags,
Minor hurdle: minor snags:
Snow starts coming, few flakes first,
More keeps coming, not dispersed.

More snow coming than predicted,
To the house we're not restricted.
Feeling good – well, not too bum.
Isabel's party – here we come!

Friday, October 13

Friday morning was a different story:
Half-foot snow and slush, by glory.
Tree limbs down from weight of snow –
Must be removed before we go.

Sue tries hard to lift a limb,
Falls on fanny, face turns grim.
Ankle screaming, hurts like hell,
Sprained or broken? Hard to tell.

Neighbor drives us to DeGraff.
"Broken, bone chip" says the staff.
Six hour later, a stranger drives us back,
A foot of snow, the house is black.

Electricity out, no heat or light,
Sue with cast and crutches plight.
New challenges all, both big and small
All because of Sue's *and* snow **fall.**

Saturday, October 14, 2006

We narrowly got out of driveway today
Per branches and limbs and snow in our way.
Out to the doctor to look at Sue's ankle.
It and the weather our schedule did rankle.

Dan and good neighbors cleared driveway for the car,
Once we got back, we weren't going far.
Still no heat or lights or power,
The start of many a perplexing hour.

Glad that my strength has suddenly returned
To face these new challenges we seemed to have earned.
Maybe lymphoma is on its way out -
Know more in December – then we can shout!!

REFLECTIONS ON WEEK 23

While my journey with lymphoma has not really ended,
The road has now taken new direction.
For six months, I've been a care receiver,
Now caregiver is the projection.

With Sue on a walker and cast on her foot,
For the broken/sprained ankle still swollen,
Attention is turned from myself to my wife,
New challenges — we'll try to control 'em.

But I figure control and direction will come
From a spirit, a God whom we trust.
We'll plod on ahead, helping others as we're led
And pass out from wear-out, not rust.

REFLECTIONS.........FROM WEEK 29
November 23 – 25, 2006

It's Thanksgiving weekend and thankful we are
For a road with so many great blessings.
The six months of chemo is now history -
And a chance to check up on progressings.

So slowly but surely my strength's coming back —
I almost feel normal again.
No hot flashes, hiccups or throat attacks now
And the Blahs even gone. Amen!

Now it's waiting and hoping that a clear CT scan
Will come up at the end of December.
Also repairing: Sue's ankle! Needs caring!
(Oh, yeah, she's my Love, I remember!)

She gave up on crutches the very first day
As the walker became helper of choice.
Before long she was gingerly putting her weight down
And walking some steps — with rejoice.

Since Spring - a long road; not as bad as it coulda-been,
I'm lucky in many respects.
With the Good Lord aboard and the Wife of my Life,
We can handle the toughest of treks.

P.S. #1

DECEMBER 26, 2006

'Tis the day after Christmas and all thru the house
This creature is tired and so is his spouse.
Glad Dave is here and family Christmas Day,
But keeping the place clean – it just ain't our way.

But since November and "No chemo no more",
Each day's a little better; that's what I waited for!
Just a tiny bit better as each day goes by,
Not quite so tired, a little more spry.

So can't help but wondering what the CAT scan will show
This Thursday for taking, next Tuesday to know.
My good Dr. "C" will give me the word.
On January 2, I will have then heard.

Good news or not so, I'll just have to wait,
Get on with my life and whatever's on my plate.
I'm thankful this journey is just about done,
Looking forward to the next – it's gotta be more fun.

P.S. #2

JANUARY 2, 2007

Finally -- time came -- to see Dr."C"
Regarding the CT scans for me.
We walked into his office, said "Here we are."
Said he to me, "You have C. R.".

I asked "What's that mean? Is it Cancer Return?
Or Coronary Relapse did I earn?
Or could it be Chronic Re-infection?
Or maybe even CAT-scan Rejection?"

"No," says he, "you have come clean,
Complete Remission is what I mean."
Then he picked me up from the office floor
And I hoped that I'd see him: nevermore!

"You will come back in four months time,
Meanwhile, enjoy your feeling prime".
Relieved and relaxed, we drove away,
Thankful for this special day.

(Cont'd)

So ends one journey, a challenge from the start,
A test of my drive, a demand of the heart.
With Sue at my side, I knew we could win;
With God as our driver, let the New Year begin.

As my strength returns and my naps decrease,
My appreciation for each day will never cease.
My focus remains: To enjoy life and smile,
Praise God and love others in my own simple style.

Bill Castle

PS #3

For a year after writing this journal, Bill Castle was cancer free. Then it returned. He faced it as he always had faced physical problems in his life - optimistically. But this time complications set in and my Bill died on April 17th, 2008.

We had known each other since 7th grade. And this year we would have celebrated our 54th Anniversary. They were wonderful years filled with love, lots of laughter, tender support for each other and our children. Our life together was a gift I will always treasure. I keep the picture you see on the back cover of this book next to my bed so his smiling face still greets me in the morning and says goodnight at the end of the day.

By now you will have discerned something about him – his humor, deep faith – but there is more. He was a joy to know and he would have enjoyed knowing you. His laugh and smile lit up a room. He was a gentle man, a humble man with a deep and abiding interest in bringing hope and inspiration to people in need of it. Indeed, I have discovered that he touched far more people than our family had ever realized.

I know you would have liked him.

Our children, Dave, Dan and Kathy and grandgirls Libby and Maggie join me in hoping that you will have found this a meaningful journey for you and your caregivers too.

Sue Castle